ÌJOBA JOURNAL VOLUME 1

WELCOME

This journal is designed to guide you through a six-month journey of spiritual grounding, agreement, and intentional growth. Each message is meant to be read slowly, reflected on prayerfully, and carried with you throughout the week.

There is no rush here.
No pressure to perform.
No comparison to others.

This is a space to meet God honestly, to listen attentively, and respond faithfully. Allow the Holy Spirit to guide your reflection, your writing, and your pace.

Published by IJOBA LLC United States of America

ISBN: 979-8-9955152-1-0

First Edition

ABOUT THIS JOURNAL

This journal is a compilation of messages written and developed through personal reflection, prayer, and study of Scripture.

Each weekly entry is rooted in biblical text and structured to support thoughtful engagement over time.

The purpose of this volume is not performance, but steady growth — to encourage consistent reflection, disciplined prayer, and deeper understanding of God's Word.

These pages are meant to be revisited, written in, and lived through.

HOW TO USE THIS JOURNAL

Each week begins with a scripture and reflection. Before journaling, read the full Bible passage in context. Sit with the scripture, allowing it to settle before moving on to the reflection.

Work through the daily prompts over the course of the week. You are not expected to answer everything at once. Write honestly. Pray openly. Pause when needed.

This journal is not a checklist — it is a companion. Let it support your walk with God, not pressure it.

Drawn by Desire, Sustained by God

Scripture: Psalm 63:1

REFLECTION

David does not come to God out of comfort or routine. He comes thirsty.

Psalm 63 is not written from abundance, but from the wilderness — a place of lack, pressure, and displacement. Yet it is there that David recognizes something essential: his deepest need is not relief, but God Himself.

This verse reminds us that spiritual hunger is not a weakness; it is an invitation. A longing for God that signals awareness — awareness that nothing else can fully sustain us. When desire is directed toward God, it becomes the very thing that keeps us grounded when circumstances are unstable.

God does not shame hunger. He meets it.

And when we seek Him earnestly, He becomes the source that sustains us beyond what the environment can provide.

What does it feel like to be "thirsty" for God in this season of my life emotionally, spiritually, or mentally?

What have I been turning to lately to feel fulfilled or steady?

Is it truly satisfying me?

David sought God early and intentionally.

What would seeking God "early" look like for me right now — not in time, but in priority?

How might God be using this space to deepen my dependence on Him?

Where am I currently in a "wilderness" season?

Where am I currently in a "wilderness" season?

CLOSING REFLECTION

Spiritual hunger is not something to fix — it is something to follow.

Called Before You Were Ready

Scripture: Jeremiah 1:5

REFLECTION

Jeremiah's calling did not begin with his confidence, experience, or agreement.

It began with God's foreknowledge.

This verse reminds us that God's calling is not reactive — it is intentional. Before Jeremiah could speak, serve, or even understand his purpose, God had already set him apart. The call came before readiness, not after it.

Often, we wait to feel equipped before we say yes. God, however, calls us while we are still forming. Readiness is not the requirement — obedience is. Growth happens after the call, not before it.

When God speaks purpose over your life, He is not asking you to prove yourself. He is inviting you to trust that He will shape what He has already chosen.

Where in my life do I feel unqualified, yet clearly called?

What fears surface when I think about stepping into responsibilities, I don't feel ready for?

God knew Jeremiah before he knew himself.

How does that truth challenge the way I define my identity or limits?

What am I postponing because I believe I need more preparation first?

How might obedience look different if I trusted God to develop me along the way?

What would change if I believed that being chosen
matters more than feeling confident?

CLOSING REFLECTION

Calling precedes confidence — God supplies what obedience unlocks and reveals.

Trusting God Beyond What You See

Scripture: Proverbs 3:5–6

REFLECTION

Following God is rarely about having clarity. It is about surrendering control.

Proverbs 3 does not ask us to understand the path — it asks us to release our dependence on our own perspective. Human understanding is limited by what we can see, predict, and measure. God's direction is not.

This passage reminds us that leaning on our own understanding often feels safer because it is familiar. Yet familiarity does not guarantee wisdom. God's guidance requires humility.

The willingness to admit that our view is partial and His is complete.

Acknowledging God in all our ways is not a passive act. It is an intentional decision to invite Him into choices, plans, and expectations. When we do, direction follows — not always immediately, but faithfully.

What situation in my life am I trying to fully
understand before I trust God with it?

Where have I been leaning more on logic, comfort, or control than on faith?

What does it look like for me now to "acknowledge God" practically in my daily decisions?

How has my own understanding failed me in the
past, even when my intentions were good?

What fear surfaces when I consider releasing control
to God?

If I trusted God to direct my path, what step might I take differently this week?

CLOSING REFLECTION

Trust begins where control ends.

Obedience Without Full Understanding

Scripture: Genesis 12:1–4

REFLECTION

God's instruction to Abram did not come with a detailed plan — it came with a direction.

"Go" was the command, not "understand."

Genesis 12 reveals an important truth about obedience: it often requires movement before clarity. Abram was asked to leave what was familiar without knowing where he was going. The promise followed the obedience, not the other way around.

We often want assurance before action, but faith operates in reverse. Obedience is not about certainty; it is about trust. When God calls us to move, He is inviting us to rely on Him rather than on the comfort of what we already know.

Obedience reshapes identity. Each step taken in trust aligns us more deeply with God's purpose, even when the outcome is still unfolding

Where is God asking me to move or respond
without giving me all the details?

What familiar places, habits, or mindsets am I
hesitant to leave behind?

How do I typically respond when God's instruction
feels incomplete or uncomfortable?

What fears surface when I consider obeying before I fully understand?

How might obedience be shaping me, even if the results are not yet visible?

What is one small step of obedience I can take today
in response to God's leading?

CLOSING REFLECTION

Obedience often opens doors that understanding cannot.

Strength Renewed in Waiting

Scripture: Isaiah 40:31

REFLECTION

Waiting is often misunderstood as inactivity, but Scripture presents it as a place of renewal. Isaiah does not say those who rush ahead will gain strength — he says those who wait on the Lord will.

Waiting redirects our dependence. Instead of relying on momentum or urgency, we learn to rely on God's timing and sufficiency. Strength is not always restored through movement; sometimes it is restored through stillness and trust.

When we wait on God, we exchange our limited endurance for His sustaining power. The renewal comes not because circumstances change quickly, but because our source changes completely.

What does waiting look like in my current season —
emotionally or spiritually?

Where have I been tempted to move ahead of God
out of impatience or fear?

How do I usually cope when progress feels slow?

What kind of strength am I currently asking God for?

How might God be renewing me through the
waiting rather than after it?

What would it look like to trust God's timing today
without resisting it?

CLOSING REFLECTION

Waiting is not weakness when God is the source.

When God Closes the Door

Scripture: Revelation 3:7

REFLECTION

Closed doors often feel like denial, but Scripture reveals them as authority in action. God does not close doors arbitrarily — He closes what no one else has the authority to reopen.

This verse reminds us that God's sovereignty protects us as much as it directs us. A closed door may feel disappointing, but it also prevents paths that would distract, delay, or diminish what God is doing in us.

Trusting God when doors close requires humility. It asks us to believe that His perspective is wider than our desire and that restraint can be as purposeful as access.

What door has recently closed in my life that I am
still questioning?

How did I initially interpret that closure — as loss or protection?

What emotions surface when I think about letting go
of what didn't open?

How might God be guarding me through this closed door?

What new direction might I be overlooking because I'm focused on what ended?

What would it look like to trust God's authority over my disappointment?

CLOSING REFLECTION

Closed doors are often evidence of careful guidance.

Chosen, Not Accidental

Scripture: Ephesians 1:4

REFLECTION

This verse affirms something foundational: your existence is intentional. Being chosen in Christ means your life is not an afterthought or a coincidence.

God's choosing is rooted in love, not performance. Long before accomplishments or failures, God established purpose. Identity, then, is something received — not earned.

Understanding this shifts how we view ourselves. When identity is grounded in God's choice, comparison loses its power and insecurity no longer defines worth.

Where do I struggle to believe that my life is intentional?

How has comparison distorted my sense of identity?

What parts of myself do I try to earn acceptance for?

How does knowing I am chosen change how I view
my purpose?

What false labels do I need to release?

What would it look like to live today from a place of acceptance rather than striving?

CLOSING REFLECTION

Identity is secure when it is received and accepted, not proven.

Refined, Not Rejected

Scripture: Malachi 3:2–3

REFLECTION

Refining is often painful because it involves exposure, not abandonment. God's refining work is intentional — He purifies what He values.

This passage reminds us that discomfort does not mean disapproval. Refinement removes what cannot last so that what is true can remain. God stays present in the process, carefully shaping rather than discarding.

Understanding refinement reframes hardship. What feels like pressure may actually be preparation.

Where in my life do I feel stretched or
uncomfortable right now?

What assumptions have I made about God's silence
or discipline?

What might God be refining rather than removing?

How do I usually respond to correction or exposure?

What areas of growth have come through difficulty
in the past?

How can I trust God's presence in this refining
season?

CLOSING REFLECTION

Refinement proves value — it does not negate it.

Examine the Heart

Abba Father,

I come to You humbly, lifting up the one who has chosen to draw near to You.

My prayer is that they would examine themselves truthfully, and that their heart would be postured to receive correction without resistance.

Where conviction is present, let it lead to repentance and not to shame.

Bring anything hidden fully into the light.

Break through any denial, pride, or self-justification, and soften their heart so it remains teachable and responsive to You.

Give them the strength not to turn away from what has been revealed, but to face it with honesty and trust in You.

In Your Son Jesus' name,
Amen

Peace That Guards You

Scripture: Philippians 4:6–7

REFLECTION

God's peace does not eliminate circumstances — it protects the heart and mind within them. This peace stands guard, not because everything is resolved, but because trust has been placed correctly.

Anxiety thrives when we carry responsibility God never intended us to hold. Prayer and gratitude redirect that weight back to Him. Peace follows not as denial, but as divine protection.

This peace is active. It guards thoughts, emotions, and reactions when uncertainty remains.

What situations currently cause me the most anxiety?

How do I typically respond when I feel
overwhelmed?

What worries am I carrying that God invites me to release?

How does gratitude shift my perspective when
anxiety rises?

How can prayer become my first response instead of my last?

What would it look like to allow God's peace to guard my thoughts?

CLOSING REFLECTION

Peace is protection, not avoidance.

Authority Comes from God Alone

Scripture: Romans 13:1

REFLECTION

Authority is not self-assigned — it is established by God. This verse challenges the way we view leadership, submission, and control.

Recognizing God as the source of authority reshapes how we respond to structure and responsibility. It reminds us that power is stewarded, not owned, and that obedience ultimately reflects trust in God's order.

This understanding brings clarity. When authority is seen through God's lens, it is no longer about dominance, but accountability.

How do I personally respond to authority — with
resistance, fear, or trust?

Where have I struggled to submit, and why?

How does knowing God establishes authority change
my perspective?

In what areas of my life do I hold responsibility over others?

How can I steward authority with humility rather than control?

What does obedience to God look like in my daily
decisions?

CLOSING REFLECTION

Authority is safest when it is rooted in God.

God Orders the Steps

Scripture: Psalm 37:23

REFLECTION

This verse does not say God orders the destination — it says He orders the steps. Direction is often revealed incrementally, not all at once. God's involvement is not distant or occasional; it is detailed and ongoing.

When we walk with God, progress does not depend on speed but agreement. Even missteps can be redirected when the heart remains submitted. God delights in the process of guiding, not just the outcome of arrival.

Trust grows when we recognize that each step matters, even the ones that feel small or uncertain.

What step am I currently on that feels insignificant or unclear?

Where have I been tempted to rush ahead instead of walk steadily?

How does knowing God delights in my path change my perspective?

What step has God already clarified that I've been hesitant to take?

How do I respond when direction unfolds slowly?

What would it look like to trust God with today's step only?

CLOSING REFLECTION

Direction is found in faithful steps, not hurried leaps.

Faith Before Evidence

Scripture: Hebrews 11:1

REFLECTION

Faith does not wait for proof — it responds to promise. Hebrews defines faith as confidence in what is hoped for, even when evidence is absent. This challenges our instinct to rely on what is visible and measurable.

Faith anchors the heart when outcomes are still forming. It does not deny reality; it trusts God beyond what reality currently shows. Evidence may come later, but faith must come first.

Walking by faith reshapes how we approach uncertainty — not with fear, but with expectation.

Where in my life am I waiting for evidence before I trust God?

What promise am I holding onto even though I can't see results yet?

How do I typically respond to uncertainty?

What has faith required of me in past seasons?

What fear surfaces when I consider trusting without proof?

How can I choose faith today despite unanswered questions?

CLOSING REFLECTION

Faith moves before certainty arrives.

Pressed, But Not Forsaken

Scripture: 2 Corinthians 4:8–9

REFLECTION

Pressure does not mean abandonment. Paul acknowledges hardship honestly yet refuses to interpret difficulty as defeat. This passage reveals a tension that believers often live in — challenged yet sustained.

Being pressed can feel overwhelming, but God's presence remains constant. What looks like breaking is often strengthening. God allows pressure without permitting destruction.

This verse reminds us that resilience is not self-produced; it is God-sustained.

Where do I currently feel pressure or strain?

How have I interpreted hardship in this season?

What truth does this scripture speak against discouragement?

How has God sustained me even when
circumstances were heavy?

What perspective shift might God be inviting me
into?

How can I remain grounded while under pressure?

CLOSING REFLECTION

Pressure does not cancel God's presence.

God Sees What Others Don't

Scripture: 1 Samuel 16:7

REFLECTION

God's evaluation differs from human judgment. While people assess appearance and performance, God looks at the heart. This truth brings both comfort and responsibility.

Being unseen by others does not mean being overlooked by God. At the same time, visibility does not equal approval. God's focus remains inward, where intentions are formed.

Understanding this frees us from comparison and anchors our worth in God's perspective.

Where have I felt overlooked or misunderstood?

How has comparison affected my confidence or joy?

What does God see in me that others may miss?

How do I evaluate myself — outwardly or inwardly?

What heart posture might God be shaping right
now?

How can I set in order my perspective with God's truth?

CLOSING REFLECTION

God's vision reaches deeper than appearance.

The Weight of Obedience

Scripture: Deuteronomy 28:1–2

REFLECTION

Obedience carries weight because it carries consequences. This passage highlights how agreement with God brings blessing, not as reward alone, but as result.

Obedience is not passive agreement; it is active response. Choosing God's way shapes outcomes, direction, and influence. Blessings come not from perfection, but from submission.

This truth reframes obedience as partnership rather than burden.

How do I typically view obedience, as restriction or agreement?

Where has obedience required sacrifice from me?

What blessings have followed obedience in my past?

What resistance do I feel when God asks for
obedience?

How might obedience be shaping my future?

What step of obedience is God inviting me into
now?

CLOSING REFLECTION

Obedience aligns us with God's design.

Strength in Weak Places

Scripture: 2 Corinthians 12:9

REFLECTION

God's strength does not eliminate weakness — it meets it. This passage reframes weakness as a place of encounter rather than deficiency.

When we acknowledge limitation, we create space for God's power to work. Weakness humbles us, keeping dependence rightly placed. Grace is not diminished by struggle; it is revealed through it.

This truth invites honesty instead of hiding it.

Where do I feel most aware of my limitations?

How do I usually respond to weakness, by hiding it
or acknowledging it?

What does this scripture say about God's grace toward me?

How might weakness be positioning me for growth?

What would it look like to rely on God more fully?

How can I shift my perspective on vulnerability?

CLOSING REFLECTION

God's power meets us where we are honest.

God Is Not Rushing You

Scripture: Ecclesiastes 3:1

REFLECTION

God works within appointed times. This verse reminds us that seasons are intentional, not accidental. Growth cannot be forced without consequence.

Rushing often stems from comparison or fear, but God's timing is purposeful. He is more concerned with formation than speed. Each season carries its own assignment.

Learning to honor timing cultivates patience and peace.

Where do I feel pressure to move faster than I should?

What season am I currently in?

How has rushing affected my peace in the past?

What might God be teaching me in this season?

How can I honor God's timing instead of resisting it?

What would it look like to be fully present where I am?

CLOSING REFLECTION

Timing shapes growth as much as action does.

Set Apart

Father God,

I continue to lift up the one who said yes to drawing near to You.

My prayer is that they would not stop here but continue forward with a surrendered heart — laying down their will and their ways for Yours.

Remind them that they are loved by You and chosen by You. Let that truth steady them as they move into this next part of the journey.

Teach them to walk in humility, understanding that this process is not about perfection, but about obedience and honesty before You.

As emotions rise and shift, help them not to be led by what they feel, but to remain grounded in who You are. Give them a deeper understanding of Your character and Your love.

Let reverence grow in them. Let them stand in awe of You, with a heart that recognizes Your holiness.

Continue Your refining work in them. Remove what does not reflect You, and shape what does.

Strengthen them to remain in Your Word and let their yes remain steady.

In the name of Jesus,
Amen

Set Apart With Purpose

Scripture: Romans 12:2

REFLECTION

Being set apart is not about isolation — it is about transformation. God's work begins inwardly, renewing the mind before redirecting behavior.

This verse challenges conformity while offering clarity. Transformation reshapes how we think, choose, and discern. God's will become clearer as agreement deepens.

Set-apart living reflects intention, not superiority.

Where do I feel pressure to conform?

How has my thinking been shaped by my environment?

What areas of my mind need renewal?

How does transformation affect discernment?

What patterns might God be inviting me to release?

How can I pursue renewal intentionally?

CLOSING REFLECTION

Transformation begins in the mind.

The Testing of Faith Produces Endurance

Scripture: James 1:2–4

REFLECTION

Testing is purposeful, not random. James reframes trials as opportunities for growth rather than interruption.

Endurance develops when faith is exercised under pressure. Maturity is not achieved by avoiding difficulty, but by walking through it with trust.

This perspective shifts hardship from obstacle to instrument, the very tool God uses to shape our character.

What trial am I currently facing?

How have I interpreted testing in the past?

What endurance might God be building in me?

How does perspective influence perseverance?

Where have I seen growth through difficulty before?

How can I remain patient during testing?

CLOSING REFLECTION

Endurance is formed through faithful perseverance.

God Finishes What He Starts

Scripture: Philippians 1:6

REFLECTION

God's work is not incomplete or abandoned. What He begins, He sustains and completes. This promise reassures us when progress feels slow or unfinished.

Growth often happens gradually. God's faithfulness remains constant even when transformation feels subtle. Completion is not dependent on our perfection, but on God's commitment.

This verse anchors hope in God's consistency.

Where do I feel discouraged about unfinished
growth?

How has God remained faithful in my journey?

What has God already begun in me?

How does this promise shape my hope?

Where do I need patience with myself?

How can I trust God's process more fully?

CLOSING REFLECTION

God's faithfulness completes what He begins.

God Hears Before You Speak

Scripture: Isaiah 65:24

REFLECTION

This verse reminds us that God's attentiveness is not reactive   it is relational. Before words are fully formed, God is already aware of the need. Prayer is not about informing God; it is about aligning our hearts with Him.

God's response is not delayed by our articulation. He listens beyond language and understands beyond explanation. This truth invites rest, especially when we struggle to find the right words.

Knowing that God hears before we speak reassures us that we are never overlooked or misunderstood in His presence.

What concerns have been weighing on my heart?

How does knowing God hears before I speak change
how I approach prayer?

Where do I hesitate to bring things to God because I feel unsure or unprepared?

What emotions do I struggle to express openly to
God?

How has God shown attentiveness to me in past seasons?

What would it look like to rest in God's assurance today?

What would it look like to rest in God's assurance today?

CLOSING REFLECTION

God's listening begins before our words do.

Led by Peace, Not Pressure

Scripture: Colossians 3:15

REFLECTION

Peace is not merely a feeling — it is a guide. Scripture encourages us to let peace rule, meaning it has authority in decision-making. Pressure often pushes us toward haste, while peace invites us into patience.

God's peace does not force or rush. It steadies the heart and clarifies direction. When choices are driven by anxiety or urgency, peace is usually absent.

Learning to recognize peace as a signal helps us distinguish God's leading from external noise.

What decisions am I currently feeling pressured
about?

How do I usually respond to urgency or expectations from others?

Where do I notice peace present — or missing — in my choices?

What might God be communicating through the absence of peace?

How can I slow down enough to listen for God's peace?

What decision needs to be surrendered to God's
guidance?

CLOSING REFLECTION

Peace clarifies when pressure confuses.

When God Says Wait

Scripture: Psalm 27:14

REFLECTION

Waiting is not passive resignation; it is active trust. This verse pairs waiting with courage, reminding us that patience requires strength.

God's instruction to wait is often an invitation to deepen reliance rather than rush resolution. Waiting builds endurance and shapes character in ways immediate answers cannot.

Choosing to wait with hope guards the heart from discouragement and impulsive decisions.

What am I currently waiting on God for?

How does waiting affect my emotions and
expectations?

What fears surface when answers are delayed?

How can I strengthen my heart while waiting?

What has waiting taught me in past seasons?

What would hopeful patience look like for me today?

CLOSING REFLECTION

Waiting strengthens trust when anchored in hope.

God Is Your Provider

Scripture: Matthew 6:31–33

REFLECTION

Jesus redirects attention from worry to priority. Provision comes from agreement, not anxiety. This passage does not deny real needs — it reframes where trust is placed.

When God's kingdom becomes central, provision follows in proper order. Worry often magnifies uncertainty, but trust anchors the heart in God's care.

God's provision extends beyond material needs; it includes peace, wisdom, and sufficiency.

What needs have been causing me the most concern?

How does worry influence my faith and decisions?

What does it mean for me to seek God's kingdom
first?

How has God provided for me in unexpected ways
before?

Where might trust replace anxiety in my life?

How can I set in order my priorities more closely
with God's promises?

CLOSING REFLECTION

Provision follows trust, not worry.

Rooted So You Don't Waver

Scripture: Colossians 2:6–7

REFLECTION

Growth requires grounding. Being rooted in Christ stabilizes faith and prevents wavering during uncertainty. This passage emphasizes consistency — walking, building, and strengthening.

Roots develop quietly, often unseen. Deep roots enable endurance when circumstances shift. Faith that is rooted remains steady even when tested.

Gratitude reinforces stability, reminding us of what God has already done.

What currently anchors my faith?

Where do I feel spiritually unstable or unsure?

How have I been nurturing my relationship with
Christ?

What practices help strengthen my spiritual roots?

How does gratitude support my faith?

What would it look like to grow deeper rather than
faster?

CLOSING REFLECTION

Deep roots sustain steady faith.

Guarding the Heart

Scripture: Proverbs 4:23

REFLECTION

The heart shapes direction. Scripture urges intentional care because inner posture influences outward life. Guarding the heart is not isolation — it is discernment.

What we allow into our thoughts, emotions, and influences matters. Guarding protects peace, clarity, and obedience.

This verse invites awareness and responsibility over inner life.

What influences currently affect my heart the most?

Where have I been careless with emotional
boundaries?

How do my thoughts shape my reactions?

What needs guarding in this season?

How can I be more intentional about what I take in?

What habits help keep my heart rooted with God?

CLOSING REFLECTION

What we protect within shapes what comes outward.

God Trains Your Hands for the Work

Scripture: Psalm 144:1

REFLECTION

Preparation is often unseen. God's training equips us for responsibility before opportunity arises. Skill, wisdom, and discernment are cultivated over time.

This verse acknowledges God as the source of ability. Training involves discipline, repetition, and patience. God develops capacity in private before calling us into public responsibility.

Trusting God's preparation builds confidence rooted in Him.

What skills or strengths is God currently developing
in me?

How do I view preparation — delay or investment?

Where has God trained me through experience?

What work might God be preparing me for?

How can I honor the training process?

What patience is required in this season of
preparation?

CLOSING REFLECTION

Preparation equips us for purpose.

Faithfulness in Small Places

Scripture: Luke 16:10

REFLECTION

Faithfulness is proven in ordinary moments. This verse emphasizes integrity where visibility is limited. Small responsibilities reveal readiness for greater ones.

God values consistency more than scale. He looks at the "very little" before entrusting us with "much". Faithfulness in what seems minor shapes character and trustworthiness.

This truth reframes everyday obedience as meaningful.

What small responsibilities has God entrusted to me?

How do I approach tasks that feel unnoticed?

Where might God be testing my faithfulness?

How does integrity show up in my daily life?

What habits reflect faithfulness?

How can I honor God in small acts today?

CLOSING REFLECTION

Faithfulness grows through daily obedience.

God Goes Before You

Scripture: Deuteronomy 31:8

REFLECTION

God's presence precedes us. This promise reassures us that we do not face uncertainty alone. God goes ahead, remains with us, and does not abandon us.

Fear diminishes when trust in God's presence grows. This verse invites confidence rooted in companionship rather than certainty.

Knowing God goes before us changes how we approach challenges.

Where am I facing uncertainty right now?

How does fear influence my decisions?

What does this scripture say about God's presence?

Where have I experienced God's guidance before?

How can I walk forward with confidence?

What would it look like to trust God's leading fully?

CLOSING REFLECTION

God's presence leads the way.

Strengthened From the Inside

Scripture: Ephesians 3:16

REFLECTION

True strength begins inwardly. This verse highlights God's work within — strengthening the inner being through His Spirit. External success cannot replace internal stability.

Inner strength sustains faith during pressure and uncertainty. God's Spirit renews, anchors, and empowers from within.

When inner life is strengthened, outer challenges become manageable.

Where do I need inner strengthening most?

How do I typically seek strength — externally or internally?

What drains my inner peace?

How can I invite God's Spirit to renew me?

What practices help strengthen my inner life?

How can I rely more fully on God's strength?

CLOSING REFLECTION

Inner strength sustains lasting faith.

FINAL REFLECTION

If you have reached this page, it means you stayed.
Not perfectly, but faithfully.

Six months of steady reflection is not small.
It forms discipline, deepens understanding, and
strengthens trust in God.

Growth is often quiet.
It happens beneath the surface before it is visible
outwardly.

If your responses are slower, more prayerful, more
grounded in Scripture — that matters.

This journal was never about finishing pages.
It was about walking closely with God.

As you close this volume, remember:

You do not graduate from obedience.
You continue in it.

Remain rooted in truth.
Remain faithful in prayer.
Remain steady in your trust.

Keep walking with Him.

Father God,

I lift up the one who has walked through this journey and remained.

Thank You for sustaining them — not in perfection, but in faithfulness.

My prayer is that what has been built in this time will not fade but continue to deepen. That surrender would remain their posture, and their desire for You would continue to grow.

Remind them that this was never the end, but the beginning of a life that continues to be shaped by You.

Let Your Word remain active in them — not just something they read, but something that lives in their heart and directs their steps.

Continue to refine them, to strengthen them, and to lead them in truth. Let their life reflect a growing understanding of who You are.

Keep them grounded, keep them steady, and keep them close.

Let Your peace guard them and let Your presence remain the place they return to daily.

We thank You, we trust You, and we honor You.

In the name of our Lord and Savior Jesus Christ, Amen